THE STORY OF THE IRISH LANGUAGE

First published in 1999 by
Mercier Press
PO Box 5 5 French Church St Cork
Tel: (021) 275040; Fax: (021) 274969; e.mail: books@mercier.ie
16 Hume Street Dublin 2
Tel: (01) 661 5299; Fax: (01) 661 8583; e.mail: books@marino.ie

Trade enquiries to CMD Distribution 55A Spruce Avenue
Stillorgan Industrial Park Blackrock County Dublin
Tel: (01) 294 2556; Fax: (01) 294 2564

ISBN 1 85635 248 X
10 9 8 7 6 5 4 3 2 1

Cover illustration courtesy of the Royal Irish Academy
Cover design by Penhouse Design
Printed in Ireland by ColourBooks Baldoyle Dublin 13

THE STORY OF THE IRISH LANGUAGE

EDWARD PURDON

MERCIER PRESS

ACKNOWLEDGEMENTS

Thanks are due to Mary Delargy of the Linen Hall Library, Belfast, Aidan Mac Póilín of the Ultach Trust, Belfast, Gearóid Ó Cairealláin of *Aisling Ghéar* and Áine Ó Cuireáin of Gael-Linn, Dublin.

CONTENTS

1 Establishment and Consolidation 7
2 Decline 23
3 Revival 36
4 A National Language? 50
5 *Inniu is Amárach* 65
6 Select Bibliography 79

1

ESTABLISHMENT AND CONSOLIDATION

The mortal wounds of Gaelic Ireland were inflicted at the battle of Kinsale in 1601, but the death agony was prolonged for most of the seventeenth century. At the time of Hugh O'Neill's last stand, Irish was the language of the country outside of Dublin and a few other British settlements, and there existed among the aristocracy and their educated associates a rich, sinewy language with a distinctive literature and centuries of sophisticated European culture behind it. The language, which scholars call Classical or Early Modern Irish, was highly developed and had for its regulation a kind of national academy in the schools of poets who approved or decried the innovations that are part of the natural growth of any speech. It was one of the oldest languages in Europe and the product of at least a thousand years of development, its age and continuity underlined by the fact that its earliest written forms though clearly different from the Irish of the period were recognisable as *ur*-forms of the contemporary usage. *Ocus* is not far from the modern *agus* (and), while most schoolchildren would accept the indicated resemblance between *con-accai in fer* and *chonaic sé fear* (he saw a man). Some words like *rí* (king), *tuath* (division) and *bó* (cow) have kept the Old-Irish spelling.

Modern scholars have identified different periods in the evolution of the language, the labels showing only slight variation. A convenient taxonomy might be:

- Ogam Irish: that of the inscriptions described below, fifth to seventh centuries AD
- Old Irish: seventh to ninth centuries
- Middle Irish: 900–1200
- Classical Irish: 1200–1600
- Modern (now standardised) Irish: 1600 up to the present

The language was of great antiquity, spoken in Ireland from perhaps the third century BC but lacking a notation for its expression in written form. Professor David Greene (1915–81), one of the modern scholars of the period, describes the date of its arrival with typical academic circumspection in his monograph *The Irish Language* (1966):

> Neither archeological nor traditional evidence is worth very much when we are dealing with language, but it seems to me that a date round about 300 BC is not likely to be more than two centuries out.

What is certain is that the language which we will continue to call Irish (reserving *Gaelic* for the descendant of Scots-Irish) was Celtic and descended from some common tongue, the existence of which we can postulate because of the knowledge of such cognate descendants as Welsh, Cornish and Breton. By the time Irish was the language of the majority of the inhabitants of Ireland it had linguistic cousins in Britain, Pictland, Gaul, Italy and northern Spain.

The language of the Britons who tried to resist the Roman invasions is known to scholars as Brittonic (or Brythonic) and though the Latin of the invaders replaced it, it survived in Cornish (which lasted till the eighteenth century) and Welsh, which is still spoken in its modern form by half a million speakers, about 20 per cent of the population. Though clearly related to Goidelic (as the ancient Celtic Irish was termed), by the time its existence was threatened by the incursion of Latin it had some notable differences.

It is customary to distinguish Q-Celts from P-Celts, the Goidelic speakers having lost the capacity (or the inclination) to pronounce initial 'p's, thus preferring what became *athair* (father) to the original Latin *pater*. Most words of the period beginning with 'p' are foreign and even St Patrick, who brought lettering as well as Christianity, had his name rendered as Coithriche. The distinction between 'p's and 'q's (which must proverbially be minded) is seen in differences between Irish and Welsh versions of some Latin words. The Q-holders (the sound soon became 'c') rendered the original *equus* (horse) as *ech* (modern *each*=steed), *quinque* appeared as *coic* (*cúig*=five). The equivalent Brittonic words were *ep* and *pump* while the redolent Irish word *mac* became *(m)ap* in Welsh.

The Goidelic language was and remains Irish, the modified vernacular forms Manx and Scots-Gaelic being offshoots which under the pressures of history developed their own related, recognisable languages from the beginning of the seventeenth century, making a kind of spiritual break from the country that had no longer any linguistic authority. Manx in its surviving (mainly religious) texts is a kind of phonetic Irish with an apparently unstandardised and odd-looking orthography. Like Cornish it is virtually extinct though, conscious of its heritage and the existence of about a hundred speakers who can speak and write *Gailck,* the island government have begun to cherish any residual linguistic traces. The street signs in Douglas, Peel, Ramsey and Port Erin and other towns are bilingual and a Manx museum in Douglas offers texts and dictionaries with such titles as *Pocket Manx.* A notable amount of the preservation was carried out by members of the Irish Folklore Commission. The sense of a mythology and a difficult but romantic language lurking somewhere nearby has done Manx tourism no harm and the meteorological recurrence of blanketing mist and soft rain can be blamed upon Manannán Mac Lir, the Celtic Neptune and presiding deity, who uses the mist as protection from enemies.

Gàidhlig remains vigorous on the western Scottish seaboard and the Hebrides with 80,000 native speakers and a verse and prose literature. The distant cousin Breton is spoken by 20,000 people while 700,000 claim the Breizh equivalent of the Irish *cúpla focail* (smattering – literally 'two words'). (This divergence in figures between active speakers and 'bilingual' fellow-travellers is, as will be made clear, characteristic of the situation in contemporary Ireland.) *Gàidhlig* had been brought to Pictland by raiders and colonists, finding a secure hold in the presence of the kingdom of Dál Riata which with growing territories in Antrim and Galloway bestrode the North Channel, the 'narrow sea', and imposed Erse upon the aborigines. The words *Erse* and *Scoti* were applied to the language and the people who brought it, driving out an older

Celtic language called by some scholars *Pretani*. Erse had ceased to exist by the mid-seventeenth century as Gàidhlig developed, surviving only as almost a sneer among the English and a source of vulgar puns in Ireland.

With the coming of Christianity the Irish achieved a means of writing down their language and although they were mainly farmers and stockmen the nature of the country with its many petty kingdoms meant that they also had often to be warriors. They had an imaginative memory of ancestors who were mighty battlers and of even older heroes who had semi-divine powers. These gods and fighting men, as Lady Gregory called them, were as real to the Irish of the early Christian era as Zeus or Venus to the Greeks and Romans, and their epic deeds were preserved orally in a vigorous prose that, safely committed to memory, could last – and did – for many centuries. The *seanchas* (traditional lore) that the Folklore Commission managed to collect, almost too late, from the old men and women of the western seaboard, were remnants of the epic tales of the various cycles adapted to modern Irish.

Oral preservation with an iterative system of

memorising implied two things: first, a reluctance, even an inability, in the keepers of the tradition to deviate from what was essentially a sacred text and second, a special mystery inevitably attached to the keepers of the tradition themselves. The textual language preserved in its original form was different from the vernacular of the majority of the inhabitants who, as years and centuries went by, handled to their own satisfaction a living, and therefore a changing, language. The groundlings who enjoyed Shakespeare's plays spoke like the rude mechanicals, not the lord and ladies. The learned class of the imminently Christian country who held this knowledge had power over ritual as well, also jealously preserved as part of their mystery. As history and especially tradition say, they were bound to supply the main resistance to the new system of beliefs. The missionaries from Britain and Gaul spoke Latin and so had to learn the vernacular of the people they intended to convert. Over the next two centuries they and their locally born neophytes devised a means of getting the orally preserved lore safely down on parchment and of using the new script to reflect the speech of the people.

Irish had already a kind of primitive script that was used mainly for inscriptions; called Ogam, the letters were represented by notches cut in stone (and probably wood, though there are no such survivals) like marks on a tally stick, as are still used for primitive computation and accounting. The alphabet consisted of strokes crossing either vertically or obliquely with a central line or cut on either side of them. The base line usually was the edge of a standing stone and the inscriptions in the examples surviving are mainly personal names in the genitive case. Such a cumbersome system though not inappropriate for lapidary memorials or labels of personal possession was useless for any other purpose; tally marks could not hope to encompass such a language as Irish at any stage of its development.

Though even a brief account of Irish grammatical forms and syntactical uses is beyond the scope of this study it is well to state that it has a complicated system of accidence. The highly inflected nature of the language in noun, pronoun and adjective declensions and in verb conjugations continued into modern times though most recent standardisation has tended to diminish it. Notable features are the absence of words for 'yes' and 'no', use being made in the answer of the verb in the question – the answer to 'Did you buy the book?' is *Cheannaigh* ([I] bought) or *Ní cheannaigh* ([I] did not buy); the existence of two verbs 'to be' – *is* which implies identity or essence and *tá* which suggests temporary position or accidental characteristics – *Is bean í* (She is a woman), *Tá an bád gorm* (The boat is blue); the usual positioning of the verb at the beginning of the sentence; a unique form of the second person singular pronoun in *tú*; and the retention of a vocative case which had an effect on personal names in Gàidhlig, producing Hamish and Iain (originally vocatives of Seumas and Eoin). Two further features of the language that have survived to modern times and have made the learning of Irish rather more difficult than many other European languages are the consonant modifications called lenition and eclipsis. Examples may be found in the effect of possessive adjectives on nouns: 'car' in Irish is *gluaisteán* while 'my car' is *mo ghluaisteán* and 'our car' is *ár ngluaisteán*.

An appropriate means for writing Irish was

developed as Irish monks adapted Roman uncial lettering to their own vernacular. The establishment of the monasteries followed quite quickly after the comparatively bloodless Christianising of the pagan Irish and the scribes produced within a hundred years or so an orthography with which the hero tales could be written down. The monk-scholars trained in Latin soon realised that the sounds of Irish, not only in its static forms neatly standardised but also in what was to be known as *caint na ndaoine* (the speech of the people), could be rendered in the Roman alphabet. There was much for them to write; not only were there the great hero-tales to be recorded but also the great codices of law, the accumulated history and the genealogies of a family-saturated people. When the holy fathers inscribed many saga tales into such collections as *Lebor na hUidre* (The Book of the Dun Cow), *The Book of Leinster* and *Lebor Gabála* (The Book of Invasions), they only slightly bowdlerised them. These tales included the *Cath Maige Tuired* (Battle of Mag Tuired), *Táin Bó Cuailgne* (Cattle Raid of Cooley), *Scéla Mucce meic Da Thó* (Story of Mac Datho's Pig) and *Fled Bricrenn* (Briciu's Feast).

Contemporary material began to be written, sometimes as marginalia on religious texts, sometimes as formal exercises in poetry. Dallán Forgaill's elegy for St Colum Cille was composed about the time of the saint's death in 597 and there are extant poetry fragments by Colmán mac Léníni who died in 604. Some of the verse was religious as befitted a learned class of monks but other work of the period was secular, showing a great sense of nature and the season's changes and some, especially those written as the period of Old Irish was coming to an end with the seismic effect of the Viking terrors in the ninth and tenth centuries, was social and satirical. This tradition of poetry persisted right through to the seventeenth century, in the output of the bardic schools – a survival from the highest rank of the ancient caste of the *aés dána* (men of art) – which were maintained by the wealthier chieftains, and existed alongside the monastic centres. They ceased to hold their premier social position and political power after the reforms of St Malachy (d. 1148) and the coming of the continental style of monastic houses.

By the beginning of the thirteenth century

a standard literary language had been forged and the distinction between the two kinds of professional poets, the *file* and the *bard*, became blurred. Originally the *file* was nearly as aristocratic as his master and was maintained out of respect and for prestige. These seers were also regarded as the possessors of old knowledge and magic, potent allies in confrontation with enemies. The belief in these shamanic powers persisted until Elizabethan times; Rosalind in *As You Like It* says in response to Orlando's filling the trees of Arden with his poetry: 'I was never so berhymed since Pythagoras' time that I was an Irish rat.' The *bard* was originally a kind of house poet, associated with a particular family, and his job was to praise his master and all his lineage. This required a considerable knowledge of past heroic deeds, which was regarded as history in those days, but the laureate was also required to devise eulogies on the occasions of victories, birthday odes, comings-of-age, epithalamiums for weddings and elegies for funerals. The verse was formal, the structure unchanged and the language preserved in a kind of literary stasis that showed remarkably little variation between 1200 and 1600, the period of Classical Irish.

The highest kind of composition was the *dán díreach* (straight poem) which was written to a strict syllabic and rhymed formula; other forms required less exacting standards but all were the product of schools staffed by members of particular families and maintained by individual Irish chieftains. The students lived in the schools from October to Easter, a part of their course being to compose poems in specific metres on allotted subjects lying alone in the dark and then to recite their work in public. They learned much more than composition, becoming the learned class and keepers of all knowledge. The course lasted seven years and the orally-taught curriculum included grammar, genealogy, law, music, medicine, *dinnshenchas* (topography), Latin and history. Some of the poems were on religious subjects and some, the *dánta grádha* (love poems), showed the influence of *amour courtois* that came with the Anglo-Normans.

They were, however, an elite, with a language product that was far from the ordinary speech of the people. Epic stories continued to be told and new, often satirical ones, were invented, and there was undoubtedly a certain amount of anonymous folk poetry and song composed outside of the schools of the poets and the banqueting halls of the chieftains. With the collapse of Gaelic Ireland and the consequent decline of the literary language, writers turned to the spoken vernacular, which by then had shown distinct dialectal variations. Some kind of interaction must have occurred between the static formal language of official literature and the language of the people which reacted (as does all speech) to time and chance. The future of Irish as a language and as a source of literature might have shown the same kind of development as did English with the growth of drama, and later the essay and the novel. These were, however, essentially urban-centred and in Ireland the cities were English-speaking as a rule. Theatres were built and publishing houses established early in the seventeenth century as if Dublin and Cork were British cities.

The history of the country from 1600 to 1850 engendered a gradual increase in the use of English and a slow diminution in the use of Irish. As the old order began to collapse so did the poets' schools, though they did not surrender without a fight. Even if the history of the country had been different, even if the native Irish had retained the sovereignty of their land, it is unlikely that such a rigorous system could have survived. Literature is essentially revolutionary and one way or another the bardic schools would have had to change or perish. As it turned out the decision was not theirs and the poetry written out of rage and despair at the change of the old order is among the finest in Irish.

2

DECLINE

The coming of the Anglo-Norman adventurers in the period 1169–1333 with their foreign language and their superior military might was to have a significant effect upon the fortunes of the Irish language, not because of any lasting damage they could inflict upon the Irish nation as a whole but because their persisting presence in the Pale meant that Ireland's integrity as a country was compromised. The descendants of the 'Gall', as the native Irish called the foreigners, may have become *Hibernicis ipsis hiberniores* (more Irish than the Irish themselves), as Archdeacon John Lynch put it in his seventeenth-century rebuttal of Anglo-Norman propaganda, but they represented a kind of colonial option which the Tudors and later dynasties were to take up. The attention of Henry VIII, the first Tudor prince, was inevitably drawn to the western neighbour because of the obvious and threatening autonomy of chieftains outside the English Pale and because of the religious adherence to Rome in Ireland of English and Irish alike.

The sixteenth-century Reformation had as much to do with power and politics as with theology and the same could be said about the European attempt to counter its effects. Yet though there were various small-scale and ultimately ineffectual attempts by Spain to aid the Irish, the perceived threat of counter-insurgency, with Ireland as a back-door entrance to those who would try to remove England's Protestant freedoms, was in fact insubstantial. To the Tudors, Ireland was rather a country of possible exploitation for the adventurers who regarded it as a colony more convenient of access than Virginia (though with equally hostile aboriginals). There may have been some who came with a view to proselytisation as well as profit but as far as the greater majority was concerned, the attempts at imposing the English Reformation were unsuccessful. Elizabeth I's publicly expressed intention of making the Irish loyal by making them Protestant was chimerical. The success of the official and unofficial plantations of Ulster during the reign of James I meant that the north-east did become Protestant in the sense that the new landholders had brought their religion with them. In spite of official government policy there was no serious attempt at conversion; in their heart of hearts the last thing the newcomers wanted was a large population of newly converted native-born Protestants free of penal disability.

An edict of Henry VIII in 1541, after he had been proclaimed king of Ireland, made the first formal pronouncement about the Irish language since the Statute of Kilkenny (1366) had attempted to prevent the greater Gaelicisation of the English colony. It enacted that 'the King's true subjects, inhabiting this land of Ireland, of what estate condition or degree . . . shall use and speak commonly the English tongue and language . . .' There is a story that may not be apocryphal that of all the Gall-Gaelach lords who were present only Ormond had sufficient English to explain the terms of the proclamation to the others.

Irish was never formally proscribed; indeed the Anglican clergy who were given the task of promulgating the reformed doctrines, especially during the reign of Elizabeth I, were required to learn Irish so that the majority could begin to understand the implications of the Thirty-Nine Articles. At the queen's behest the College of the Holy Trinity was established in 1592 with the intention of educating Irish youth, and William Bedell, who was provost from 1627 to 1629, made sure that the divinity students learned something of Irish. The library of Trinity became the safe repository of many of the priceless Irish manuscripts including the *Book of Kells* (8th century), the *Book of Leinster* (12th Century) and the *Book of Durrow* (*c.* 650). Elizabeth was just as astute as her father and infinitely more patient. It was during her reign that the power of the Anglo-Irish earldoms was effectively destroyed and with the so-called Flight of the Earls four years after her death in 1603, Ulster, the last outpost of Gaelic civilisation, was left virtually leaderless. By then an Irish translation of the New Testament (1602) in the approved version as *An Tiomna Nua* was already in use and Thomas Cranmer's *Book of Common Prayer* was printed in 1608 as *Leabhar na nUrnaightheadh gComhchoidchionn*.

The rest of the century was marked by increasing social upheaval and the gradual displacement of Irish as the language of political jurisdiction and culture. With remarkable prescience, four Franciscan brothers of the friary at Bundrowse, County Donegal, compiled between 1632 and 1636 *Annála Ríoghachta Éireann* (Annals of the Kingdom of Ireland) which attempted to tell the whole story of Ireland from the earliest days until the unhappy present. Similarly Seathrún Céitinn (*c.* 1580–*c.* 1644), a secular priest and poet from Tipperary completed *Foras Feasa ar Éirinn* (*Groundwork of Knowledge of Ireland*) an indispensable work in Gaelic historiography.

In the years that followed the coming of the Anglo-Normans, the poets had come to terms with the Anglo-Irish lords and attached themselves to their houses as praisers, genealogists and scholars as contentedly as they had done with the Irish chieftains. Now, conscious as few others that a cataclysmic change had come upon their world, their seventeenth-century successors tried with only minimal success to find patrons among the new men. Musicians were still welcome at the great feasts but the songs they sang to the harp were unintelligible to the unlettered British. The destruction of the Irish aristocracy was a gradual process (with occasional periods of acceleration, such as the penal enactments after Cromwell had finally put paid to the Catholic Confederacy). The Cromwellian land settlement claimed eleven million acres, approximately 55 per cent of all the Irish lands and although things improved a little after the Restoration and in the brief reign of James II, by 1704 the native Irish owned only 14 per cent of the land of their own country.

The dismay at the loss not only of revenue but also of prestige is palpable in the literature of the period. The attitude of the Irish men of letters to the newcomers is summarised in *Pairlement Chloinne Tomáis*, an anonymous prose satire in two parts, the first prophetically written *c.* 1600 in parody of the characteristic genealogies, and the *Lebor Gábala*, the second after the Cromwellian settlement, excoriating the boorishness and illiteracy of the new landowners. Such poets as Dáibhí Ó Bruadair (1625–1698) and Aogán Ó Rathaile (1675–1729) have left bitter attacks on the louts (as it seemed to them) who replaced the old aristocracy who spread the grey wing upon every tide after Limerick. When his patrons the Fitzgeralds left for France, Ó Bruadair, who was a trained bard and highly educated, had to work for a time as a farm labourer. His poem *'Mairg nach fuil 'na dhubthuata'* (A pity not to be an utter boor) is a brilliant vituperation but also a lament for a lost age. Ó Rathaile's 'Vailintín Brún', a poem addressed to a possible new patron to replace the MacCarthys, shows remarkable disdain from a beggar.

The poets were the Irish equivalent of Hamlet's 'abstract and brief chronicles of the time' and a special form, the *aisling* (vision) was devised by the seventeenth-century poets as a kind of prayer of hope in which Ireland comes to the poet in a dream as a beautiful maiden and is assured that she might one day be restored to her former greatness with the help of the Stuarts. Even before Charles Stuart's defeat at Culloden in 1746 the poets, now scattered and having to survive as teachers, army recruits, subsistence farmers and menials, had wisely discounted Stuart help but in their *aislingí* still believed that Gaelic Ireland would one day be restored. As the bleak eighteenth century proceeded and the full bite of the Penal Laws was felt, the poets still acted as Irish-speaking Ireland's sages, pamphleteers and satirists. The bardic schools were gone, as were most of the great establishments that had supported them, but the ancient lore had not been lost. Just as in former times the presence of an *ollamh* (master-poet) was enough to constitute a school, so the surviving poets held their own much reduced but still active schools. Such poets as Seán Clarach Mac Dónaill (1691–1754) of Charleville, County Cork, and Seán Ó Tuama (1707–75) and Aindrias Mac Craith (1710–90) from Limerick maintained the tradition of the *cúirt éigse* (court of poetry), the first holding a regular 'showcase' session in his house at Kiltoohig. New work by established figures was read and discussed, and young poets were encouraged to submit their work for critical approval. When Mac Dónaill died, Ó Tuama summoned all the southern poets to a *cúirt* at Croom to consider how poetry and indeed the Irish language might be preserved.

The poets of the 'hidden Ireland', as their historian Daniel Corkery called them, might have lost caste but their poetic talents and their age-old powers to 'raise blisters' with their satire had not deserted them as the superb *Cúirt an Meánoíche* (*The Midnight Court*) (1780) by Brian Merriman (1749–1805) shows. The 1,206-line poem not only gives a brilliant picture of the rural Ireland of its time but was in its feminism and its denunciation of prevailing male celibacy (including that of priests) quite shocking. Its language, structure, Rabelaisian tone and parodic elements show not only an informed appreciation of a thousand years of Irish poetry but also of the European tradition of the Courts of Love.

One large body of material, known as *filíocht na ndaoine* (the poetry of the people) consisted of anonymous folksong and poetry, often of great beauty and far from primitive. Much of it took the form of love songs and it bridged the dark years and provided a portable literature for those who had no other. The songs stopped; as

Sir George Petrie (1789–1866), the archaeologist, put it in one of the most chilling remarks about the Great Famine of the 1840s: the population had forgotten how to sing.

By then, too, the language had lost its intellectual position; it was no longer the speech of those with power, wealth or influence. As Maureen Wall put it in her 1966 Thomas Davis lecture, 'The Decline of the Irish Language':

> . . . the Irish language had been banished
> from parliament, from the courts of law,
> from town and country government, from
> the civil service and from the upper levels
> of commercial life.

It did persist in the rural areas of the south and west though it lacked cultural potency because, thanks to social and political events, a majority of the monoglot population had become illiterate. The poets who tried desperately to keep the language alive and maintain a kind of literature were essentially a diminishing body of learned men who could not rely on continuing respect from their unlearned clients. As Gerard O'Brien

Pillarstone with Ogam inscriptions, Coolnagort, Dunloe, County Kerry
(Office of Public Works)

Key to Ogam in the Book of Ballymote, 14th and 15th centuries
(Royal Irish Academy)

Iryſhe,	Latten.	Engliſhe,
Conneꝛtatu	Quomodo habes.	How doe you.
Taim go maih.	Bene ſum.	I am well,
Go po maih agad.	Habeo gratias,	I thancke you,
In eol oꝛt gealaſg	Poſſis ne ~~~	Canni you ~~ }
Do laꝺuꝺio.~~	hibernice loqui	ſpeake Iryſhe
Abaiꝛ laꝺꝺen.	Dic latine.	Speake Latten
Dia le pꝛiuꝺan ꝛ	Deus adiuat~~	God ſaue the }
raꝛoma ~~~	Regina Angliæ	Queene off
		Englande:

16th century Irish/Latin/English phrasebook compiled for Queen Elizabeth of England

(283)

Aiꝛ bac an oꝛ n do bj agolc
maꝛ peulc aiꝛ aꝛoꝛg do bj
'ꝛa paꝺꝛꝛg ꝺa byajcyea aꝺꝛeac
ꝺo béaꝛea ꝺo ꝛeaꝛc ꝺon mnaoꝛ.
Dꝛiꝺeaꝛ Fjonn aꝃ jaꝛpajꝺ ꝛꝃeꝛꞁ
aiꝛ mnaoꝛ ꝛeꝛmb na cꝛꝛac nôiꝛ
Dyjaꝛpajꝛ mo pjꝛ ꝺon ꝛꝛꝛꞁ nꝛil
an byacajꝺ cꝛ mo chojꝛ ꝛa cojꝛ?
Ann ꝺo ꝛejlꝛ iꝛ chbꝛl mo ꝛpeꝛꞁ.
ꞁ iꝛ ꝛhaca mé ꝺo bé chojꝛ
a Rꝛ na ꝛeꝛꝛ e ꝛan caꝛ
ꞁ meaꝛa ljom ꝛac mo ꝛꝛil
An É ꝺo céꝛle ꝺo ꝛuajꝛ báꝛ
a jꝛ꞉ean claꝛé, no ꝺo mac
no caꝺ É an ꝛac ꝛa byꝛl ꝺo eꝛꝛj
ajꝛꝺjꝛ cꝛjiꝛ ꝛ ꝃlꝛe ꝺꝛeach
No caꝺ aꝛ abꝛꝛl ꝺo byꝺn
a ajꝛꝛja bꝛ na mbaꝛ mꝛn
no an ꝛéꝛꝛjꝛ cꝛyꝛcacc (aꝛ ꝛjonn)
ꞁ ꝺubach ljom ꝺo bejc maꝛ chjm
Fájl oꝛ n ꝺo bj ꝛo mo ꝛlajꝛ
ꝺo pájꝺ jꝛ꞉ean bꝛ na byolc ꝛéꝛjꝛ
cꝛcjm ꝺom laꝛ꞉ ꝛan cꝛꝛeaꝺ
aꝛ ꝛjꝛ máꝺbaꝛ ꝺa bejc jbpꝛjꝛ
ꝛeaꝛa naꝛ ꝛhꝛlajꝛꝛ laoch
cꝛꝛꝛm ꝺo cjonn a Rꝛ na byꝺꝛan
maꝛ cꝛuꝛajꝛ mꝛhaꝛnne cuꝛam cajꝛ aꝛ
cꝛc ꝛe heaꝛ na ꝛꝛeaꝺ nꝛꝛan
Nꝛoꝛ ꝛhulajꝛꝛ Fjonn cuꝛ na nꝛeaꝛ
cꝛác eꝛꝛ bé aꝛaꝛb ꝛo na eꝛeꝛ ꝃléꝛc
éuajꝺ ꝛo bꝛuaé an loéa ꝛúám
á ꝛhupajꝛleam mna na mbaꝛ ꝛ péꝛꝺ.

O o 2   Do

Extract from Charlotte Brooke's 'Reliques of Irish Poetry' (1789),
containing a section of the Ossianic poem 'Laoi na Seilge'
('The Ballad of the Hunt')
(Trinity College Dublin)

Tadhg Ó Murchú, collector with the Irish Folklore Commission, recording
on the ediphone in Spuncán, Waterville, County Kerry, *c.* 1936
(Roinn Bhéaloideas Éireann)

Periodical publications, 1882–1968
(Government Publications)

THE TREE OF LIFE.

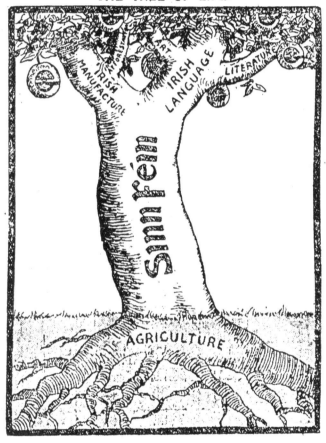

'The Tree of Life', *Sinn Féin*, Dublin, 13 March 1911
Balancing the commercial branch, the cultural branch of Sinn Féin's
nationalist vision reflects its committment to the preservation of Irish and
the creation of art and literature in Irish

shows in his essay 'The Strange Death of the Irish Language, 1780–1800' (1989), the last two decades of the eighteenth century were crucial in the determination of whether the decline should be serious but temporary or virtually terminal.

A combination of the following factors all but finished Irish as anything other than a 'provincial patois': the growth of urbanisation; improvements in communications and the exposure to outside influences of what had been closed and self-sufficient monoglot communities; increased bourgeois prosperity and consequent anglicisation among some native speakers; the Catholic Church's decision to opt for general anglicisation with no provision for Irish in the new seminary in Maynooth (1796); the attentions of the antiquarians who wished to preserve Irish as a fascinating relic; the association of *spoken* Irish with 'drunkenness, idleness and improvidence' and a lack of respectability about having any knowledge of it; the need of access to English as the language of contracts and other legal documents and in forensic pleas; the apolitical nature of Irish society which diminished the need for the solidarity of a shared and exclusive language; the requirement of English for a whole range of public sector employment and in the various armed forces; and, as the century turned, the implicit (specific in the case of Daniel O'Connell) suggestion of the country's new political leaders that lack of English was somehow a bar to political and material progress.

O'Connell used Irish when it suited him but as he wrote to his friend W. J. O'N. Daunt:

> Therefore although the Irish language is connected with many recollections that twine around the hearts of Irishmen, yet the superior utility of the English tongue, as the medium of all modern communication, is so great that I can witness without a sigh the gradual disuse of Irish.

Yet at the height of O'Connell's influence the population of Irish speakers was at least two million, about 30 per cent of the population. By then with the system of National Schools where English was the medium of education in place and the strong support for anglicisation among parents with not exclusively utilitarian motives meant that the monoglot population would steadily diminish. The effects of the Great Famine of the 1840s and the mass emigration which followed from what had been mainly Irish-speaking areas meant that by the 1891 the Irish speakers numbered no more than 680,000 and apart from the inhabitants of remote pockets, as in the Sperrins in County Tyrone, the Bluestacks in central Donegal and some of the offshore islands, they were bilingual. Why so many failed to retain their Irish and why succeeding generations did not maintain bilingualism remains a difficult question and one for which there are no satisfactory – or honourable – answers.

3

REVIVAL

It is convenient to see the stir of cultural activity that characterised the last decade of the nineteenth century as filling the vacuum left by the fall and death of Parnell in 1891 and as a high-minded reaction to the ugliness of the mutual recriminations among the Irish politicians of the time. Though such institutions as the Gaelic Athletic Association (1884), the Irish Literary Theatre (1899) and the Gaelic League (1893) were independent of each other and not always on friendly terms, they all drew their considerable energy and popularity from a lively spirit of change and a sense of national identity that characterised the period. The ebullience showed if nothing else that the trauma of the Famine and the massive emigration that followed was passing. The success of the Land League agitation and the power of the Irish Parliamentary Party in Westminster had given those nationalists who cared about such things a new sense of hope. Being Irish in Ireland was no longer a condition but a role. And with the renewed interest in Ireland's cultural past and a growing sense of independence in Irish games and pastimes, for some enthusiasts the time seemed ripe to make a move for restoration of Ireland's own language.

Revival was a word that those who at the very end of the nineteenth century tried to restore Irish as the national language tended to eschew since it implied a kind of exhumation, a resurrection as from a grave. The aims of the Gaelic League on its foundation, as stated in an early pamphlet (1896) were two: the *preservation* [emphasis mine] of Irish as a national language and the extension of its use as a spoken tongue; and the study and publication of existing Gaelic literature and the cultivation of a modern literature in Irish. The founders' declaration of the existence of a living language which would be used as the basis for an effective modern language, able to handle the technical vocabulary of twentieth-century life, gave a new significance to the *Gaeltacht* (areas where Irish was the first language), although its inhabitants were on the whole rather indifferent to the movement.

The League was the most successful and persistent of a number of earlier initiatives that gave it a foundation upon which to build. (All such are called *reamhconraitheoirí* – League precursors – as though they were preparing the way for the language Messiah.) Significant among them was the Society for the Preservation of the Irish Language (SPIL) which had been founded in 1876 by David Comyn (1854–1907), who was a clerk in the National Bank. It campaigned successfully for Irish to be accepted as a subject for the Intermediate Certificate examination and produced some necessary if rather dull text books. In 1882 there came, in the words of Máirtín Ó Cadhain in an essay 'Conradh na Gaeilge agus an Litríocht' (1972), *'an gnáthghalar Gaelach, scoilteadh'* (the chronic Irish disease, a split). The faction led by Comyn formed *Aontacht na Gaeilge* (The Gaelic Union) which produced an important bilingual magazine, *Irisleabhar na Gaedhilge* (*The Gaelic Journal*). It was for this periodical that Fr Peter O'Leary (1839–1920), a native speaker from West Cork, known universally as *An tAthair Peadar* wrote part of his novel *Séadna*, one of the first books in modern Irish.

The literary aims of the Gaelic League were a recognition that for about 250 years the language was 'topless'; there had been no significant national writing or publishing and, wanting these, it was without power or prestige. English was strong: it was the language of the schools and third-level institutions, commerce, law, social intercourse, theatre and popular periodicals. Some new initiative was required to counter this ascendancy. Douglas Hyde (1860–1949), who took the chair at the first meeting of the League at 9 Lower O'Connell Street on 31 July 1893, had already drawn attention to the need, as he saw it, for 'de-Anglicising the Irish People'. He had made this the theme of his presidential address to the National Literary Society the previous November. As he said with unanswerable logic, 'We have no business condemning the English as the scourge of the country while we are at full bent to imitate these same English.' The ideal of de-Anglicisation should be attained 'through the language, through the music, through national games, but especially through the language and through speaking the language.' Hyde, who as a sickly son of a Roscommon manse, had learned his Irish from 'the company of old countrymen' (as Yeats put it in *Autobiographies* [1956]), had come to prominence as a friend of Lady Gregory and a peripheral player in the Literary Revival. His Protestantism, though entirely unselfconscious, emphasised from the start the non-sectarian character of the League.

The other significant member of the committee was John MacNeill BA (1867–1945) (as he is termed in the minutes of that first meeting – later he was to change his first name to Eoin) who became secretary. He had been born in Glenarm, County Antrim, and at the time of the founding of the League was working as a law clerk in the Four Courts. He knew no Irish until he was an adult and found that he learned more on short visits to Inis Meáin than from all his book study. That he had already formulated (at least in outline), the method which was to make the League the most successful of all the agencies of language restoration is evident in two articles: one written for *The Irish Ecclesiastical Record*: 'Why and How the Irish Language Is to Be Preserved' (December 1891), and the other for *Irisleabhar na Gaedhlige*: 'A Plea and a Plan – for the extension of the movement to preserve the Gaelic Language in Ireland' (March 1893), which was written in Irish with an English translation.

MacNeill's latter article was forcefully rather than elegantly written, being a series of principles stated in near-syllogistic form:

- The Gaelic is now spoken by nearly, if not quite, 700,000 persons in Ireland.
- The districts in which Gaelic is spoken amount to fully one-third of the area of Ireland.
- It is therefore possible to preserve the Gaelic language, and if it is not preserved, the fault is ours.

The need to preserve Irish where it was spoken as a first language meant that attention was to be focused on the Gaeltacht, the coastal regions

from Malin Head to Waterford. The speech of
the Gaeltacht, though by now strongly dialectal,
was to be the basis for the modern Irish language
rather than the elaborate, almost courtly relics,
that had been the interest of the scholars.
Cainnt na ndaoine (the spoken vernacular) was
chosen because it was an existing if limited
language and it was from those regions that the
adult teachers should come. MacNeill was
supremely conscious that new methods of teaching had to be devised since the people who were
to learn Irish were adults, a majority of whom
had left school at fourteen or younger. Moreover,
he never had much confidence that Irish would
be restored by teaching in the schools.

Eventually a system known as the *modh
díreach* (direct method), a modified form of
Berlitz, was found to be the most appropriate.
Classes were conducted entirely in Irish and,
though exhausting for the teacher and frequently
confusing for the pupil, the method worked,
largely because motivation was strong in the
early years of the League. A sentimental relic of
the period were the *Ceachtanna Simplidhe* (Easy
Lessons) in four volumes devised mainly by Fr

Eoghan O'Growney (1863–99) who had been an early member of SPIL. Most people were able to master quite quickly the lessons in Volume I which sold 20,000 copies in the year 1899–1900, because they were *too* easy and many who had assimilated the material regarded themselves as Irish speakers – and caused a distortion in the 1921 Census! Hyde records in his book *Mise agus An Connradh* (The League and I) (1931) that the sale of subsequent volumes was considerably less. The often grotesque and rustic simplicity of the *ceachtanna* caused a certain amount of amusement in sophisticated circles. Susan Mitchell, in her book on George Moore (1916), referred to Volume I rather loftily as 'the manual that instructed our young Gaelic enthusiasts to "Put the butter on the floor" or recorded the unnatural thirst of "Art" who went so often to the well.' The books were far from perfect but as Leon Ó Broin wrote in *Studies* (Winter 1963) ' . . . they were absolutely necessary tools in the hands of the new organisation.'

The source of the living language was, of course, the Gaeltacht where it was spoken instinctively and unselfconsciously. It was also an obvious source of the teachers who would have linguistic authority. The trouble was that many of these were illiterate in Irish, some not even able to read it. If they were to be successful adult teachers they needed to be trained in methodology and basic classroom techniques; the *modh díreach* had to be assimilated. *Coláistí Samhraidh* (summer schools) were established in the three dialectal areas, Munster (Ballingeary, County Cork, 1904), Connacht (Tourmakeady, 1905) and Ulster (Cloughaneely, County Donegal, 1906) where the students might have access to native speakers and ordinary conversational practice might be available socially after class. (Such Donegal writers as Séamus Ó Searcaigh and Sean Mac Meanmain received their first formal education in Irish at Cloughaneely.) By 1910 there were eight summer colleges (and winter schools in Belfast and Dublin with native speakers on the staffs). Soon the majority of Irish-speaking areas from Inishowen to Ring had busy summers and when in the 1920s all teachers were required to have some competence in Irish the colleges were able to continue their (suitably modified) work.

The classes were set up by League organisers

called *timirí* (messengers) and arranged for
múinteoirí taistil (travelling teachers) to hold
classes in particular areas, often several in one
night, travelling mainly by bicycle as 'The Man
on the Wheel', a tributary poem by Alice
Milligan (1866–1953) makes clear:

> We will while away the time with fiddle,
>   and dance, and song;
> 'The way,' they say, 'is rough and the
>   school too far to reach.'
> But wait – a stir at the door and in
>   through the jostling throng
> Comes the man skin-drenched from his
>   wheel who has said he would come to
>   teach.

Milligan was an Omagh Protestant and Ulster
organiser for the League. She was the editor
(with Ethna Carbery) of the Belfast nationalist
literary magazine, the *Shan Van Vocht* (1896–9)
and was responsible for the first piece of dramatic
writing in modern Irish which was staged at the
Aonach Tír Chonaill in Letterkenny in 1898. It
was about St Patrick's struggle with the druids

at Tara and was characteristic of the way the League used all possible media in the cause. The *aonach* (cultural assembly) in Letterkenny was typical of the festivals of music, verse and dancing that the League sponsored. The first Irish play as such, was the perennial favourite *Casadh an tSúgáin* (*The Twisting of the Rope*) by Hyde using his wonted pen-name *An Craoibhín Aoibheann* (the pleasant little branch). He was to write eight other plays in Irish, including the satirical bilingual *Pleusgadh na Bulgóide or The Bursting of the Bubble* (1903), an attack on the Trinity doctors, Mahaffy and Atkinson, who had said that where Irish literature was not religious it was silly and where it was not silly it was indecent. At the time when drama was being forged in the smithy of Elizabethan and Jacobean England, Irish writers had other preoccupations but once the tradition of plays in Irish was established it became an important part of the movement.

The first *Oireachtas* was held on 17 May 1897. The word is still used for the Irish legislature but also has the meaning of 'festival'. It was an annual showcase and progress report at which prizes were awarded for, among other things, writings in Irish, which were then published in a Proceedings volume. These grew thicker as more and more competitors contributed. Typical of the event was the award in 1899 to Edward Fournier of £2 for a vocabulary of weaving terms employed by the tweed trade in south Donegal. It was an Oireachtas prize that encouraged Padraic Ó Conaire (1882–1928), one of the finest of Irish short-story writers, to give up his job with the Post Office in London and begin his Connacht travels. The Oireachtas, like the Welsh *Eisteddfod* and Gàidhlig *Mod* upon which it was partly modelled, was also a super example of the *feiseanna* (music festivals), those gatherings that were supposed to be modelled on the ancient Gaelic musical festivals. These had done more than anything else to make the country aware of the League's existence and have proved to have been the most successful and most long-lasting of the original initiatives.

The League also produced a weekly newspaper called *Fáinne an Lae* (*The Dawn*) which first appeared on 8 January 1898, price 1d. That edition contained an editorial called 'Teanga na hÉireann' ('The Language of Ireland') and a profile of Hyde. The paper lasted until March 1899 when the editor Bernard Doyle resigned over a dispute about subscriptions and it was replaced by the much longer lasting *An Claidheamh Soluis* (1899–1930). That title meant 'the sword of light' a recurrent symbol in Irish folklore, a memory, anthropologists said, of the first sight of a glint of steel in the Bronze Age. Patrick Pearse (1879–1916), who was to lead the Easter Rising, became editor in 1903 and it was in the issue of 1 November 1913 that Eoin MacNeill wrote the editorial 'The North Began' which was essentially the throwing down of the gauntlet by the Irish Republican Brotherhood to the anti-Home Rule Ulster Volunteer Force and a statement of intent of the formation of the armed Irish Volunteers. It also showed how far the League had moved from the non-sectarian, non-political character of its foundation.

It was naive of such non-aligned members as Hyde to think that a language movement which was not that of the administration and specifically the speech of a pre-colonial Ireland was not essentially a political movement as well. Such

separatism was in those years as logically revolutionary as Yeats's play *Cathleen Ni Houlihan*,
that in the playwright's words may have sent out
'certain men the English shot'. Certainly after the
formation of the UVF in 1913 the League became
plangently committed to armed struggle. When in
1915 a motion at the *Ard-Fheis* (AGM) committed
the League to 'a free Gaelic-speaking Ireland',
Hyde found it necessary to resign as president. By
then, however, the League had made a considerable
social as well as linguistic impact. It became an
effective pressure group, succeeding in making St
Patrick's Day a national holiday (though it also
closed the pubs) and insisting, not without some
bitter controversy, that Irish be a compulsory
subject for matriculation in the new National
University of Ireland (1908). In spite of the
League's efforts, Irish was not re-established as the
country's language but the efforts of its members
made vigorous if limited bilingualism a real
possibility. As Desmond Fennell wrote in *Twentieth
Century Studies* (1971), 'It would be a rash man
who would shout his secrets in Irish from any
window in any Irish town.'

4

A NATIONAL LANGUAGE?

With the setting up of Saorstát Éireann in 1922 the principles advocated by the Gaelic League became government policy. Irish was recognised as the first official language and all aspects of administration were handled bilingually. Irish was part of primary and secondary school curriculums, became a compulsory subject for the Intermediate Certificate in 1928 and for the Leaving Certificate in 1934, and would remain so until 1973. (The following year it ceased to be compulsory for civil service examinations.)

The new state had its troubles, mainly financial, and the treasury department became notorious for its fiscal puritanism. (This parsimony was to become a habit and resulted, for example, in so important a cultural medium as Radio Éireann which had been founded in

1926, being starved of resources for many years. This meant, among other things, that a precious store of folk music and *seanchas* was nearly lost because of lack of personnel and proper equipment and precious archival material was destroyed for lack of space or because the discs had to be reused.) The new Minister for Education was Eoin MacNeill and he still had no confidence in the ability of the schools to restore Irish. Things were fine as long as the children were at school – although the methods of teaching did little to establish conversational fluency – but the language of the country was still in fact English. It was notably the language of debate in the Dáil and of commerce. The lip service to Irish reached a kind of congealment and it was customary for news-papers up to the end of the 1950s to begin reports of public speeches with some such formula: 'Speaking in English and in Irish Mr de Valera said . . .' when in fact the Irish may not have amounted to anything more than an introductory *'A chairde Gaeil'* (Irish friends). As J. J. Lee puts it rather trenchantly in *Ireland 1912–1985* (1989):

A knowledge of Irish was made compulsory for certain state posts, but no genuine attempt was made to gaelicise either politics or the civil service, prerequisites for the success of the revival ... The essential hypocrisy occurred less in the area of compulsory Irish in the school than in the failure to provide opportunity, or obligation, for the regular use of Irish subsequently. The refusal of all governments since the foundation of the state to practise what they preached alerted an observant populace to the fact that the revival was a sham.

The policy of compulsory Irish in schools did produce a limited bilingualism; children with good teachers can be taught anything. The trouble was that for too long the definition of a 'good' teacher was one who had 'good' Irish with sometimes little regard paid to general pedagogic skills. This led to an untested belief that native speakers dominated the teaching profession because of their undoubted facility in Irish and that lesser competence in other subjects was winked at. Teachers became concerned too at the educational policy, gradually introduced, of teaching other subjects 'through the medium' as it was called – it inevitably led to the pun 'through the tedium' – and an INTO (Irish National Teachers' Organisation) survey in 1941 came to the conclusion that it led to some educational retardation in the pupils. (Fifty or more years later, after many redefinitions of education it is hard to know just what 'retardation' may have meant then. At a period of high emigration to Britain in spite of the war perhaps it was felt that the study of science and mathematics using Irish nomenclature was inappropriate for potential workers in munitions and other industries.) Since 1939, however, most primary and secondary teachers were recognised by the Department of Education as competent to teach through Irish and the education imparted was *in practice* as good as that in say Northern Ireland schools.

Certainly policies of what might now be called 'positive discrimination' such as giving extra marks to children who answered examination questions through Irish were of doubtful equity and again seemed to give an unfair advantage to those from Gaeltacht areas, though no one commented upon the fact that very few Gaeltacht parents could afford secondary education for their children. This imbalance could be defended as a necessary aid to areas of social deprivation. Between 1922 and 1939 the number of native speakers fell from 200,000 to 100,000. Emigration, a countrywide problem, was acute in the subsistence areas where Irish had been preserved. The need was not for linguistic conservation; the language held and as the modern world began to penetrate the areas of first language it adjusted to new demands. The problem of jealous defence of dialect continued and many native speakers (most living in Dublin and other cities) whether from Munster, Connacht or Donegal affected to despise as *ersatz* the locutions of government agencies as they struggled to find translations for the vocabulary of Irish life which was becoming increasingly modern and urbanised. Though strongly resisted by diehards outside the Gaeltacht, the standardisation of grammar and spelling in the 1950s seemed to establish it as a contemporary language at last and the publication of a normative English–Irish dictionary by Tomás de Bhaldraithe in 1959 did much to increase the language's capacity to handle modern terms. This maintenance of an up-to-date lexis is now the responsibility of the *Coiste Téarmaíocht*, a body set up by the Department of Education (now 'and Science') and monitored by the Royal Irish Academy.

The more serious Gaeltacht problem was correctly seen as conservation of population and this was to be achieved by industrial development by state agencies. These initiatives worked, in that the rate of erosion in population of Gaeltacht areas was slowed down and the numbers engaged in non-agricultural employment increased. With the obstinacy with which society resists logical solutions to sociological problems, however, the number of Irish speakers continued to fall even though the Gaeltacht areas ceased to be the most underprivileged in the country. The 1981 census showed that the Gaeltacht areas contained only 2.3 per cent of the population and 7.4 per cent of Irish speakers. And all but the most sanguine accept that this leaching away of the numbers of native speakers will continue but at an undramatically slow rate. All native speakers are bilingual, and the future of the Irish language is likely to be as an extra possession, a useful addition to the Hiberno-English that will be the normal means of discourse, of a slowly increasing minority of the total population of the island as a whole.

The restoration of the language was not achieved with the coming of the new state but the picture was not all gloom. A significant modern literature began to appear – and be subject, it must be said, to the same censorship that afflicted writing in English. This was partly due to the power of the Catholic Church, the often worse anticipatory censorship of the laity trying to avoid possible future clashes with the clergy and a policy of moral protectionism (and self-regard) that characterised all aspects of the state until the end of the 1960s. One serious problem about Irish books was the regionalism that two centuries without a national literature had spawned. Grammar, pronunciation and even vocabulary differed in detail. The divergence was summed up in the following chauvinistic epigram which the Young Irelander Thomas

Davis (1814–45) mentioned in an essay on the possible restoration of Irish written for the *Nation*: *Tá blas gan ceart ag an Muimhneach; tá ceart gan blas ag an Ultach; níl ceart ná blas ag an Laighneach; tá ceart agus blas ag an gConnachtach* (The Munster person's speech is tuneful but inaccurate; that of Ulster is accurate but tuneless; the Leinster people's speech has neither flavour nor accuracy; the native of Connacht has both accuracy and tunefulness). The acceptance in 1927 of a new government-subsidised revised edition of the *Foclóir Gaedhlige agus Béarla* (Irish–English Dictionary), the marvellously rich but Munster-biased masterpiece first published in 1904 by Fr Patrick Dinneen (1860–1934), simply ignored the problem.

An attempt was made to make the Munster form the standard largely because of the limpid language and popularity of An tAthair Peadar's *Séadna* (1904), a Munster version of the Faust legend. This plan was thwarted by the fact that the more successful books in Irish came from Connacht and Ulster (and that O'Leary's West Munster Gaeltacht showed signs of much greater shrinkage that elsewhere). Padraic Ó Conaire wrote in Connacht Irish and it was typical of the time and personalities that Fr O'Leary had objected to his urban novel *Deoraidheacht* (1910) as indecent. He agitated that it be dropped from the syllabus, saying that he would never have supported the campaign for Irish in the matriculation examination if he had known what immorality it would lead to. Connacht also produced in time the poet Máirtín Ó Díreáin (1910–88) from Inis Mór in the Aran islands and the novelist Máirtín Ó Caidhin (1906–70), whose *Cré na Cille* (1948), a pattern of voices of the dead in a Connemara graveyard, is as fine an Irish novel as any written in English. The work of these two writers needs no special pleading nor mitigation of critical attention; it stands on its own feet as literature requiring neither sentimental nor nationalistic emotional subsidy. Liam O'Flaherty (1896–1984), also from Inis Mór, well known as a brilliant, if maverick, writer in English, returned to his first language with *Dúil* (1953) a collection of powerful short stories, some of them redactions of earlier English ones. A consideration of these versions is not only a lesson in translation but also a fascinating comparison of two remarkably different languages. It is convenient here also to mention the work of the Cork poet Seán Ó Ríordáin (1917–77), who broke new ground in his verse while still showing a deep attachment to the tradition. Both for his own poetry and for his influence on many younger practitioners, he is regarded as the modern master in his chosen field of literature.

The Government of Ireland Act (1920) had created the state of Northern Ireland by carving six counties out of Ulster's historical nine and the third of the population of the new state that was Catholic and nationalist was effectively downgraded to second-class citizenship. The one-party Unionist government, which was to last for slightly more than fifty years, was, when its leaders bothered about the question of the Irish language, vehemently anti-Irish, regarding its very existence and nationalist insistence upon having it as a school subject as an affront and clear potential of subversion. They did not wish, however, to be seen to come down too heavily. As Lord Charlemont, the Stormont Minister of Education said in 1933, ' . . . forbidding it under pressure will stimulate it to such an extent that the very dogs – at any rate, the Falls Road dogs – will bark in Irish.' Irish ceased to be taught during paid school hours in primary schools but it was eventually tolerated as a foreign language and as such was an acceptable subject in secondary schools. It became virtually compulsory in Catholic schools with recognition for scholarships to third-level and with an inspector to maintain both teaching and learning standards. By the 1950s, when the General Certificate of Education replaced the old Senior Certificate, so many pupils were regularly entered for Irish that, as with French, the oral and dictation examinations required two sessions. (The Ministry of Education was reasonably tolerant, providing papers in standard as well as Ulster Irish for a few schools who opted for the majority form.)

Linguistic politics were also part of the language scene in the North. The Irish that the Unionist government described as a foreign language might almost have been that to the urban Irish speakers in the Free State. The activists (with rare exceptions not native speakers) concerned to preserve their own brand of essentially Donegal Irish had the extra stimulus of opposition. By the mid-1920s the Gaelic League, its original purpose largely fulfilled in the Free State, had begun to show signs of deterioration, especially in Northern Ireland. It too was feeling the effects of partition. In consequence Lorcan Ó Muireadhaigh (1883–1941), a priest of the archdiocese of Armagh, took it upon himself to call together interested parties to form a body to be in essence the Gaelic League of the North.

The meeting was held on 3 November 1926 at Armagh City Hall. Ó Muireadhaigh had already established in 1924 *An tUltach* (native of Ulster), a monthly journal written in Ulster Irish and, once identified as its founder, received full backing when he proposed the establishment of the Ulster organisation with the deliberate purpose of preserving the northern dialect. *Comhaltas Uladh* (Ulster [governing] body), the new committee's name, represented *Sean-Chúige Uladh* (the old province of Ulster) which meant all the lands north of a line from the Erne to the Boyne and thus including County Louth. Ó

Muireadhaigh had been born in Carlingford in
that county and for a number of years had been
organiser of Coláiste Bhríde, an Irish summer
school in Omeath (until then a Gaeltacht)
which finally closed in 1924. Conscious of a
desire to preserve and to educate a new gener-
ation in the Ulster dialect, Ó Muireadhaigh
then established a college in 1926. The site
chosen was at Rannafast in the Rosses district
of west Donegal and the name of the original
County Louth college was preserved. About
fifty students attended the first course at the
new Coláiste Bhríde. *Comhaltas Uladh* went on
to do excellent work in their cleverly-defined
Ulster in the promotion of the Irish language.
By 1958 there were 151 registered branches,
their spirit remaining loyal to the ideals of the
founders.

The choice of Rannafast was judicious; just
as Connacht had produced Ó Conaire, that
district, noted for the idiomatic excellence of its
Irish, was the birthplace of two writers from the
same family, Séamus Ó Grianna (1889–1969)
and Seosamh Mac Grianna (1901–90), the
difference in names being evidence of a family

feud. The elder brother who wrote as 'Máire' (the name of his talented mother) was responsible for many novels and volumes of short stories notably *Caisleáin Óir* (1924) and *Cioth is Dealán* (1927) and was paid the accolade of parody by Myles na Gopaleen, one of many avatars of Brian O'Nolan (1911–66) in *An Béal Bocht* (1941). Seosamh's work, notably the story collection *An Grá agus an Ghruaim* (1929) and *An Droma Mór* (1969), is superior as literature and, like those of the Connacht masters, is judged as such.

Another perhaps unexpected source of Irish literature which was to preserve a record of a vanished way of life was the work of the writers from the Great Blasket, the inhabited island of an archipelago off Dunquin in County Kerry. Because of its isolation, the island had been visited by many Celtic scholars and one old islander Tomás Ó Criomhthain (1856–1937) was persuaded by a Kerry scholar Brian Ó Ceallaigh to write about his life and place. The result was *Allagar na hInise* (1928) and *An tOileánach* (1929), translated as *The Islandman*, the latter a triumph of Irish prose and a vindication of the value that the Gaelic League had put upon *caint na ndaoine*. Other islanders were inspired to record their stories: Muiris Ó Súilleabháin (1904–50) produced *Fiche Bliain ag Fás* (*Twenty Years A-Growing*) in 1933 and Peig Sayers (1873–1958) wrote her life story as *Peig* (1936). Though the Blaskets authors wrote of a vanishing (now vanished) life, the fascinating material was rendered with such linguistic elegance that not only do their books form a valuable historical and sociological archive but they proved again that Irish was as viable for literature as any other world language.

5

INNIU IS AMÁRACH

According to the 1996 census, 41 per cent of
the population claim to use some Irish and 10
per cent speak it fluently. The number of
people who have some understanding of it and
thus might with advantage listen to or view
Irish programmes on RTÉ, Raidió na Gael-
tachta and Teilifís na Gaeilge is probably very
much greater, especially since the latter provides
subtitles in English or Irish as the need arises
– and thus acts as an informal teaching agency.
Among these 'passive' clients we may place a
number who because of lack of conversational
opportunity, personal disinclination or because
their ability in Irish falls inevitably short of
that in English, rarely speak Irish but read it
regularly. In the Ireland that is racing towards
an míle bliain no one can reasonably complain

of lack of books, films, plays or programmes in Irish. TnaG (pronounced Teenagee), as the Irish channel is universally called, has had the same divisive effect upon the interested population as most other effective initiatives since the prospect of a modified restoration of Irish became a possibility. Each new scheme, official or otherwise, for the furtherance of the use of Irish was greeted with a perhaps intemperate enthusiasm by language activists who too often and too obviously regarded their cause as a *moral* crusade, part of the religious baggage of 'any true Irishman or Irishwoman'. This in turn tended to produce an often virulent opposition with temperature levels high and debates that descended to vituperation on both sides. The opponents of language initiatives list as objections: financial considerations (as in Matthew 26:7, 'This ointment might have been sold for much and given to the poor'), elitism, minority interest, bad educational practice, quixotry in a Europe where English is fast becoming a millennial *lingua franca* and many other cogent considerations.

Yet in correspondence columns and radio

and comment programmes, these logical reasons often seem to be irrelevant; there appears to be present some deeper psychological objection, as if the old social stigma that the Gaelic League had to fight so hard against was still attached to the language or perhaps that a mixture of a folk-memory conscience and a sense of exclusion from a privileged enclave was the true source of the opposition. The enthusiasts were, it must be admitted, frequently arrogant, exclusivist and puritanical to the extent that the term *gaeilgeoir* (Irish speaker or learner) could often be used pejoratively. They were even dismissed, mainly in large urban centres, as 'thaw shays', a rendering of *Tá sé* (It is), the beginning of many Irish sentences. The observed tendency for Irish institutions to fragment seemed to reach epidemic proportions in those involved with the language. This was most clearly seen in the resistance mounted by pressure groups to standardisation of grammar, syntax, orthography and basic vocabulary. However, with the publication in 1958 of *Gramadach na Gaeilge agus Litriú na Gaeilge: An Caighdeán Oifigiúil* (Irish Grammar and Orthography: Official Standard) and *Foclóir*

Gaeilge–Béarla (*Irish–English Dictionary*) edited by Niall Ó Dónaill (1908–94) in 1977 much of the divisiveness disappeared. A recent (1995) pocket dictionary edited by Séamus Mac Mathúna and Ailbhe Ó Corráin of the University of Ulster happily lists the Irish words for microchip (*micrishlis*), software (*bogearraí*), meltdown (*leá*) – and potato crisps (*brioscáin phrátaí*).

In truth, a large portion of the population now monoglot in English regards the 'language question' as little more than a minor irritation when they consider it at all. The end of compulsory Irish may not have been the disaster it might have seemed. Perhaps using Lord Charlemont's logic the thing to do was to ban Irish and wait for the natural contrariness of the nation to insist upon speaking and learning it. It was the spirit of the then European Economic Community (EEC) and the end of Ireland's cultural and sociopolitical isolation, rather than activities of such bodies as the Language Freedom Movement, that brought about the change. The belief, firmly held by parents, that Irish was a virtually dead language and one of no economic or commercial value compared with French,

Spanish or German had at least the effect of establishing these as curriculum subjects in schools where they were unheard-of up until then. The same parents must, however, have wondered at the efficacy of these 'modern' languages when they came to consider, if ever they did, just how useful economically the few residual phrases were to their children. They might very well have been able to order *Eiersalat und Milch* successfully in an Imbißstube in München (an unnecessary feat since *all* German waiters speak English) but they know little of Goethe and less of Heine.

The present state of the language 105 years after the founding of the Gaelic League is one of reasonable bilingual health and, the counter-apologists aside, general tolerance. Though government interventions were not always done with the tact or wisdom that might have made them more effective, later administrations learned from old mistakes as did several independent lingual agencies. One often criticised but essentially worthy operation was *An Gúm* (The Scheme), set up in 1925 by Ernest Blythe (1889–1975) to make sure of a supply of Irish textbooks and other reading material. At the beginning investment was low, the fabric quality of the books produced uninspiring and the agency not known for its speed or efficiency; Seosamh Mac Grianna's fine novel *An Droma Mór* (1969) lay in a drawer for thirty-six years. Though some original material was produced, including work by Mac Grianna, Ó Criomhthain and Ó Caidhin, most of the output consisted of translations from English and other languages. The translations were excellent and so was some of the material, notably the appropriate *Islanders* (1928) by Peadar O'Donnell (1893–1986) as *Muintir an Oileáin* and *Pêcheur d'Islande* (1886) by Pierre Loti (1850–1923) but most was either fustian stuff like *The Pit Prop Syndicate* (1922) a detective story by Freeman Wills Croft (1879–1957), a Dublin engineer, or versions of long English children's classics like Sir Walter Scott's *Ivanhoe,* translation of which seemed devoid of commonsense since they were better read in the original. It did provide some financial support for Irish-language writers and had published over 1,000 books by 1950. It continues to operate but is better funded and has a more enlightened policy.

Bord na Leabhar Gaeilge (The Irish Books Board) is a government financed agency set up in 1952 to promote by subsidy the publication of books in Irish. It now assists publishers to produce up to eighty volumes a year. Poetry and fiction continue to be written with remarkable work from poets such as Máire Mhac An tSaoi (b. 1922), Biddy Jenkinson (b. 1949), Gabriel Rosenstock (b. 1949), Nuala Ní Dhomhnaill (b. 1952) and Cathal Ó Searcaigh (b. 1956) and novelists and short story writers such as Seán Mac Mathúna (b. 1937), Breandán Ó hEithir (1930–90), Liam Ó Muirthile (b. 1950) and Séamus Mac Annaidh (b. 1961). Other significant writers, mainly of non-fiction (though writers in Irish rarely stick to one genre) are Alan Titley (b. 1947), Cathal Portéir (b. 1956) and Padraig Ó Snodaigh (b. 1935), the latter also known as the head of Coiscéim, a major publishing outlet for Irish books. Sáirseal agus Dill, founded by Sean Ó hEigeartaigh and Bríd Ní Mhaoileoin in 1945, was also a significant Irish press; their *Nuabhéarsaíocht* (1950), an anthology of modern verse, and *Nuascéalaíocht* (1952), a corresponding volume of stories, confirming the existence, in

spite of expressed disbelief, that there was a vital
literature in Irish. Its work continues as Sáirseal
Ó Marcaigh. It is also notable that some
participants in the contemporary burgeoning of
Irish publishing in the majority language carry
some works in Irish in their lists.

Drama in Irish is not neglected though
Ernest Blythe's insistence during his period of
management of the Abbey Theatre (1941–67)
upon Irish-speaking actors probably lost the
national theatre some talents, and the yearly
Irish pantomimes did not advance the cause of
literature much. He did support the Galway
Irish theatre *An Taidhbhearc* (founded 1927)
which still continues to present Irish plays. A
drama agency *Comhlachas Náisiúnta Drámaíochta*
(National Drama Association) serves the same
purpose as the British Drama League does in
Britain. The recently formed *Aisling Ghéar* (clear
vision) – the name coming from the first two
words of a famous poem 'Mac an Cheannaí'
(The Redeemer's Son) by Aogán Ó Rathaile, is
a nationally subvented professional theatre company associated with Cultúrlann Mhac Adaim
Ó Fiaich in Falls Road, Belfast. There have

been successful plays by Mairéad Ní Ghráda (1899–1971), Criostóir Ó Floinn (b. 1927) Aodh Ó Dónaill and many others, and it should be recalled that the opening production in An Taibhdhearc in 1927 was *Diarmuid agus Gráinne* by Micheál Mac Liammóir. A recent successful Abbey tour of the bilingual *Caoineadh Airt Uí Laoghaire* (Lament for Art O'Leary) by Tom MacIntyre (b. 1931), based upon the eighteenth-century poem by Eibhlín Dubh Ní Chonaill, suggested that in the sphere of drama bilingualism may be the character of the future.

Periodicals in Irish over the years had about the same lifespan as English equivalents but *An tUltach* (1924), *Comhar* (1942), the journal of *An Comhchaidreamh*, the University Association of Irish speakers, and *Feasta* (1948), published by the Gaelic League, still survive. Newspapers, *Inniu*, *Amárach*, *Anois* have come and gone. There is currently an Irish-language Sunday called *Foinse* (fountain) and a new monthly journal *Cuisle* (pulse). These are subvented by Bord na Gaeilge, a government body which acts as a financial and general purposes committee for language concerns. Also, the *Irish Independent* and *The Irish Times* in Dublin and the *Irish News* and the *Andersonstown News* in Belfast carry regular features in Irish. *Lá* (day), a broadsheet newspaper, is published each Thursday by the Belfast Cultúrlann. There are also academic journals such as *Eriú*, *Celtica*, *Éigse* and *Béaloideas*, the journal of the Department of Folklore in University College, Dublin.

One notable initiative was Gael-Linn which was founded in 1953 by Dónall Ó Mórain (b. 1923). Its purpose was the same as many other bodies but it brought an unusual energy and the modern approach associated with the changed Ireland of the 1960s. Money was obtained by a Gaelic football pool (the title means Irish Pool) – though now its main source is by government grant – and it interested itself in the production of films: *Mise Éire*/I Am Ireland (1959), *Saoirse?*/Freedom? (1961) and records (now CDs). It maintains a number of summer schools for children, specialises in specially tailored courses for vocational groups of adults and runs a highly successful yearly arts festival for children called *Slógadh* (gathering).

In Belfast, which as E. M. Forster once

memorably wrote, ' . . . stands no nonsense and lies at the head of Belfast Lough', a move to remind northern Protestants of their own Gaelic past is gaining momentum though with less than exponential growth. This recommendation to the majority is part of a general attempt at the depoliticisation of the language and in the remit of a governmental initiative, the Ultach Trust, which is headed by Aodán Mac Póilín. The word 'Ultach', here an acronym for 'Ulster Language, Traditions and Culture', is also, of course, the Irish name for an inhabitant of the northern province.

Perhaps the most interesting development in the language movement is the increase in the number of Gaelscoileanna (Irish schools). These are schools in which Irish is the language of education and through which *all* subjects including English are taught. In 1972 there were eleven primary and five secondary schools providing education through Irish outside Gaeltacht areas; in 1998 there were 124 primary and twenty-six second-level schools. Of these fourteen primary and two secondary are in Northern Ireland, with nine of the primary and one of the secondary schools receiving assistance from the Department of Education there (negotiations are continuing for finance for the Derry Meánscoil). The number of pupils attending these NI schools was 1,213 in the academic year 1997–8. (In the same year there were more than 600 at Naí-scoileanna infant schools.)

The reasons for such growth are various; a certain amount of the language interest in the North has undoubtedly to do with the troubles there and the perceived arrogation by the IRA of Irish as their exclusive possession. (This association with paramilitaries is a minor cause of disapproval of the work of the Gaelscoileanna in the north and of a holding back from association with the language movement of some who might otherwise support it.) A number of pupils in Bunscoil Phobal Feirste in Andersonstown and in Bunscoil na bhFal, both in west Belfast and in Bunscoil Cholm Cille, Derry are from known IRA families and while they are probably not a majority they do increase the proportion of working-class pupils in the northern schools compared with the largely middle-class background of most of the children in the

South. The parental motivation in many cases will not be different from that in the rest of the country. (The Gaeltachts of Rath Carn in County Meath and in Shaws Road in Belfast are still vigorous, and Cathail Ó Donnaighle, at present development officer for Irish medium education in Northern Ireland, has plans to establish a new Irish-speaking community in County Tyrone.) As Hiberno-English, that exotic product of language loss and instinctive linguistic ability, shows, Irish (mixed with Lallans in the north-east) is still close to the minds and tongues of the inhabitants of the island. Irish needs no defence; its 2,500-year history and its shaping of the psyche are too powerful to subdue: as the Ulster poet Louis MacNeice (1907–63) put it (in a related context): 'The woven figure cannot undo its thread.'

The announcement by David Blunkett, Minister for Education and Science, in October 1998 that Irish would become a recognised subject on the national curriculum in Britain has been greeted with satisfaction and a slightly cynical and very exaggerated expressed wish by language enthusiasts that it be so also in Ireland!

The Irish of the diaspora are very likely in a mixture of nostalgia and pride to wish to claim this irreducible part of their heritage. In his introduction to *Traits and Stories of the Irish Peasantry* (1830), William Carleton (1794–1869), the Irish-speaking son of native speakers, recalled what his mother said about the translation into English of 'Bean an Fhir Rua' ('The Red-Haired Man's Wife'): 'I will sing it for you; but the English words and the air are like a quarrelling man and wife: the Irish melts into the tune, but the English doesn't.' That quarrel is still going on; it is paradoxically to the country's advantage that it continue.

SELECT BIBLIOGRAPHY

Ball, M. J. (ed.) *The Celtic Languages*. London.
1993.

Connolly, S. J. (ed.) *The Oxford Companion to
Irish History*. Oxford, 1998.

Corkery, D. *The Hidden Ireland*. Dublin, 1924.
_____. *The Fortunes of the Irish Language*.
Cork, 1954.

Greene, D. *The Irish Language*. Dublin, 1966.
_____. *Writing in Irish Today*. Dublin, 1972.

De Fréine, S. *The Great Silence*. Dublin, 1965.
_____. 'Irish as a Literary Language: Past
Present and Future' in Nic Craith, M. (ed.)
*Watching One's Tongue: Issues in Language
Planning*. Liverpool, 1997.

Hindley, R. *The Death of the Irish Language*.
London, 1990

Mac Póilín, A. (ed.) *The Irish Language in
Northern Ireland*. Belfast, 1997.

Mac Mathúna, S. & Mac Gabhann, R. *Conradh
na Gaeilge agus an tOideachas Aosach*.
Indreabhán, Contae na Gailimhe, 1981.

Maguire, G. *Our Own Language*. Belfast, 1990.

Mc Mahon, S. & O'Donoghue, J. (eds.) *The Mercier Companion to Irish Literature*. Dublin & Cork, 1998.

Ní Mhuiríosa, M. *Réamhconraitheoirí*. Dublin, 1968.

O'Brien, G. 'The Strange Death of the Irish Language, 1780–1800' in O'Brien, G. (ed.) *Parliament, Politics & People*. Dublin, 1989.

Ó Cuív, B. *A View of the Irish Language*. Dublin, 1969.

Ó Cúlacháin, C. *Tobar na Gaeilge*. Dublin, 1980.

Ó Fearaíl, P. *The Story of Conradh na Gaeilge*. Dublin, 1975.

Ó Riagáin, P. 'Reviving the Irish Language' in Nic Craith (1997) *op. cit.*

Ó Tuama, S. (ed.) *The Gaelic League Idea*. Cork, 1972.

Pritchard, R. M. O. 'Language Policy in Northern Ireland' in *Teangeolas* No. 27. Dublin, 1990.

Welch, R. (ed.) *The Oxford Companion to Irish Literature*. Oxford, 1996.

Willemsma, A. & Mac Póilín, A. *The Irish Language in Education in Northern Ireland*. Ljouwert, The Netherlands, 1997.